Antique Embroidery

Compiled by Martha Campbell Pullen, Ph.D.

Book Team

Book Design
Kelly Chambers

Antique Drawings Illustrated by
Kris Broom

Editor
Joanna Pullen Hammett

Photo Stylist
Claudia Newton

Photography
Jennifer & Company, Huntsville, AL

© 1998 Martha Pullen Company, Inc.

Printed by
The C. J. Krehbiel Company, Cincinnati, Ohio
Library of Congress Catalog Card Number 98-68426
ISBN 1-878048-18-X

Martha Pullen Company has a catalogue featuring books, patterns, magazines, French and English laces, Swiss embroideries and batiste, American batiste, silk dupioni, Gotz dolls and accessories and many sewing notions. For a copy of this catalogue send $2. Martha Pullen produces *Sew Beautiful* magazine, with over $650 worth of patterns and designs in one year's collection (6 issues). Sew Beautiful has women's fashion sewing, hand and machine embroidery and classic heirloom sewing. Martha Pullen also imports three Australian magazines, *Machine Embroidery, Creative Machine Embroidery with Jenny Haskins* and *Australian Embroidery and Cross Stitch*. Martha Pullen designs embroidery computer disc designs for all sewing machines. For seventeen years, Martha Pullen has conducted the Martha Pullen School of Art Fashion in February and July of every year.

Martha Pullen Company, Inc.
518 Madison Street • Huntsville, AL 35801 • 1-256-533-9586

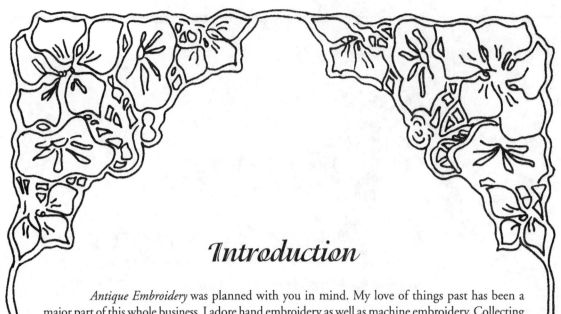

Introduction

Antique Embroidery was planned with you in mind. My love of things past has been a major part of this whole business. I adore hand embroidery as well as machine embroidery. Collecting antique books with embroidery designs has been a passion of mine for over 25 years. In planning this very special book for you, I searched through my whole collection and Kris Broom traced the ones which we thought were the most perfect for hand embroidery or for machine embroidery.

In the stitch instructions, we have included both silk ribbon embroidery instructions as well as surface instructions, some of which are identical. Fifty one stitch instructions are included. You have our permission to use any stitches for any of these embroideries, of course. Use your creativity and please enjoy this book.

I received a letter from Miss Ann R. Mills Price telling me of her wonderful "box" of embroidery designs that her mother had collected through the years. Some of the designs were from newspapers and some were the perforated kinds which had to be "traced" originally by putting tiny pencil dots in the holes. With the magic of photocopying, we didn't have to go to that extreme to prepare them for you. Miss Price gave me the box of designs with her best wishes that I would treasure them and share them with people who loved embroidery. Part of these designs are gifts from Miss Price.

Julia Rhodes has given me several things which have had a large impact on this business. She gave me the combing coat which hangs on the set of *Martha's Sewing Room*, our PBS television series. She gave me the book, *Fancywork*, by Mrs. Pullan (written in the mid 1850's) which inspired our *Fancywork* section in *Sew Beautiful*. She gave me a collection of *Lady Godey* and *Peterson Magazines* from which several of the designs in this book are taken. I thank Julia Rhodes for her gifts which I have had the privilege of sharing with you.

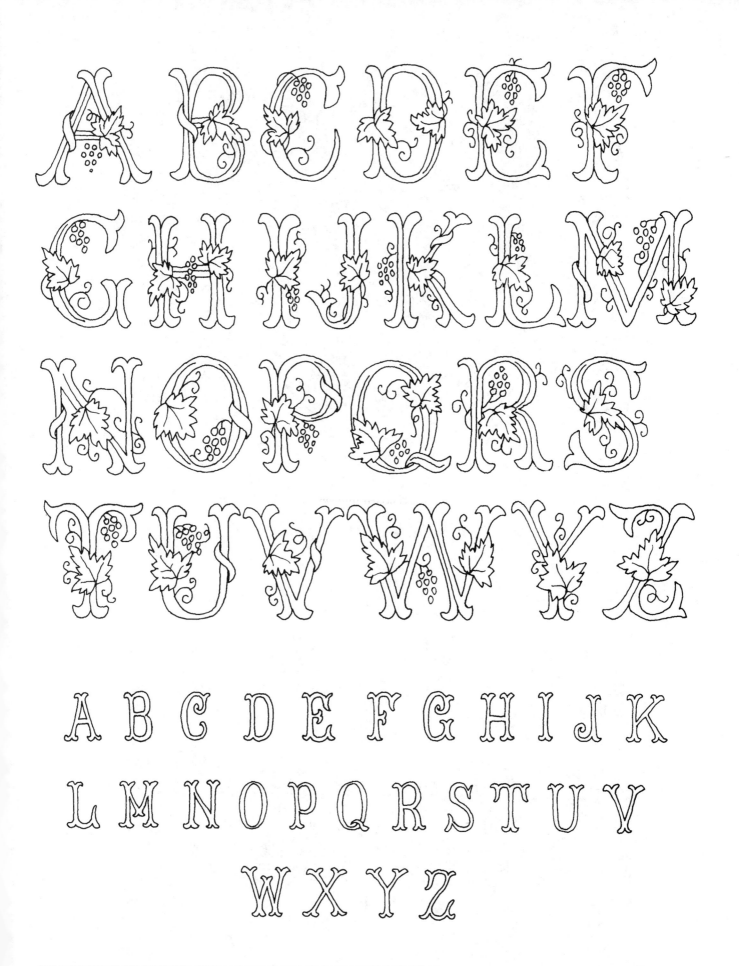

Graham's Magazine

- 1856 -

Graham's Magazine

- 1856 -

Insertions

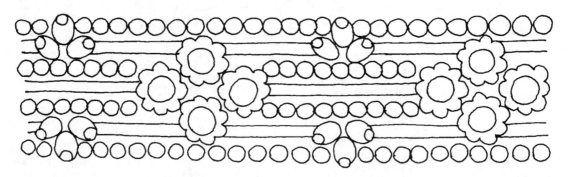

Edging

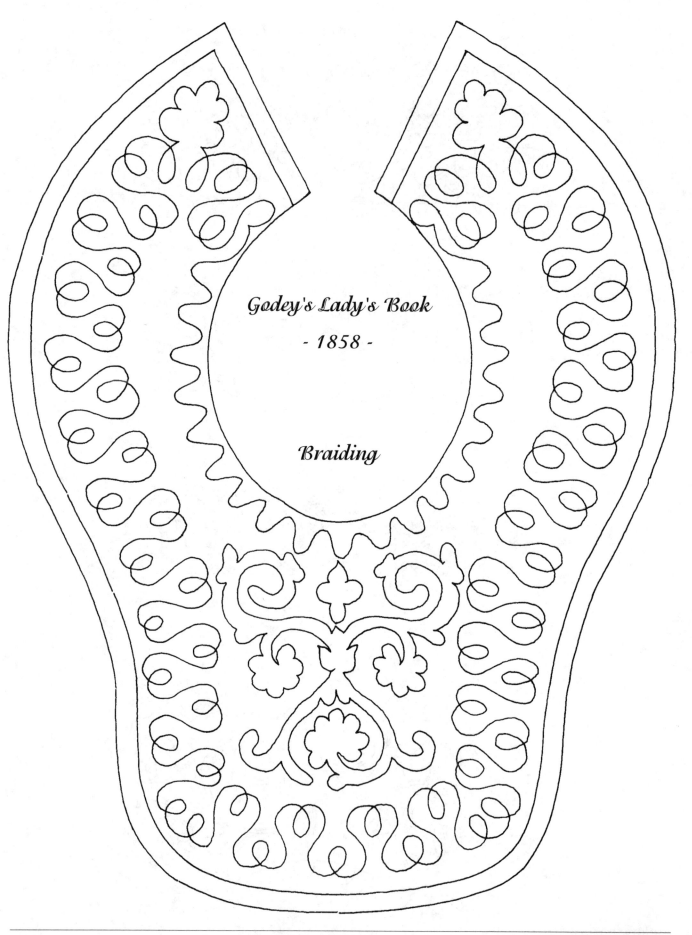

Godey's Lady's Book

- 1858 -

Braiding

Godey's Lady's Book

- 1858 -

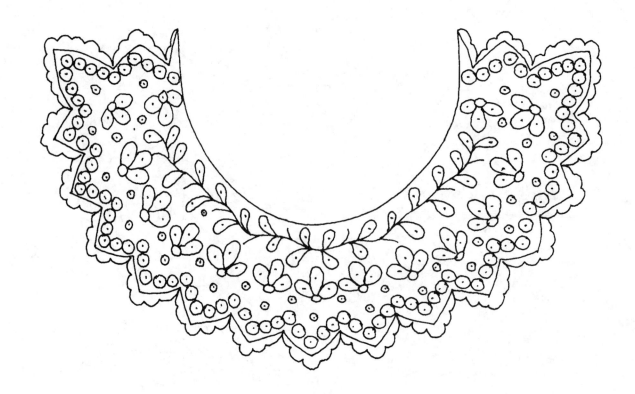

Godey's Lady's Book

- 1858 -

Peterson's Magazine

- 1866 -

from

Ingalls' Fancy Work Book

- established in 1878 -

Night Dress Designs

Ingalls' Fancy
Work Book
- established 1878 -

Wallachian Picture Frame Designs - enlarge 150%, or as desired

"Wallachian Embroidery is one of the newest, and the most popular embroidery of the season. It has already found many admirers, because it is simple, new, quickly worked, and pretty. The characteristic of this embroidery is the common Buttonhole Stitch. The stitches run from the center line to the edge of each leaf or petal, the purl coming on the edge. The Buttonhole Stitches may be slightly slanted towards the top of the petals, so as to turn the corners nicely. Sometimes the centers of the rings are punched with a stiletto, and the needle is put each time into the hole thus made. Or the center of the rings is filled in with French knots.

The use of washable foundation rings has been introduced to do away with the flatness of the original work. If rings are used for the round figures in the design, then a few padding stitches should be run in near the outlines of the leaf portions, so that they will also have a raised appearance." - *Ingalls' Fancy Work Book, 1878*

Roman Embroidery

"This design is in the Roman style, and would serve for a variety of purposes.
It may be carried out in white embroidery, in application of batiste or muslin or any other rich material."

Designs in White Embroidery

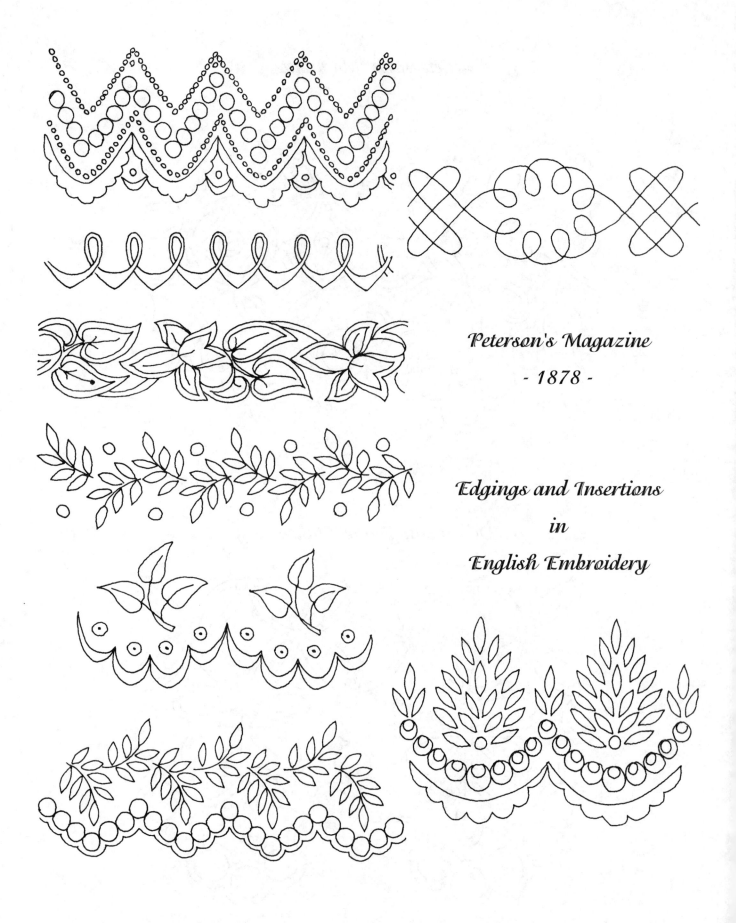

Peterson's Magazine

- 1878 -

Edgings and Insertions

in

English Embroidery

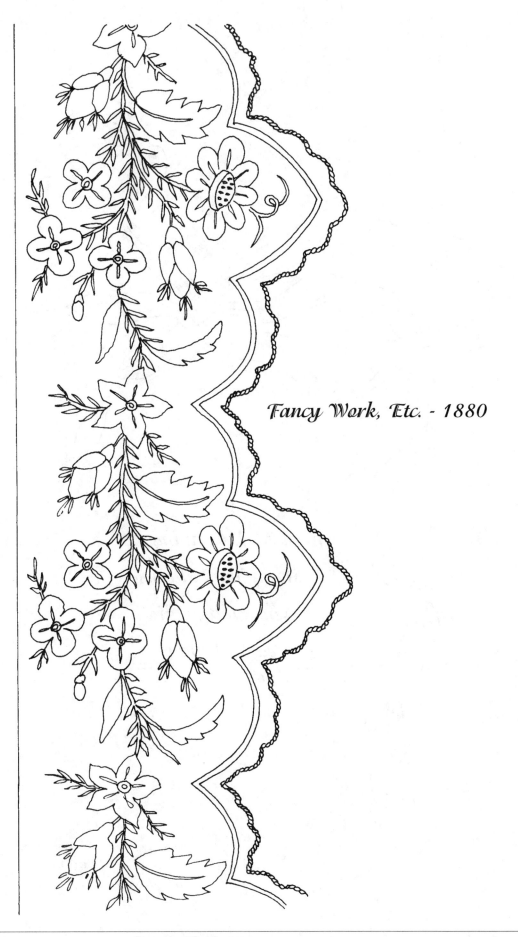

Fancy Work, Etc. - 1880

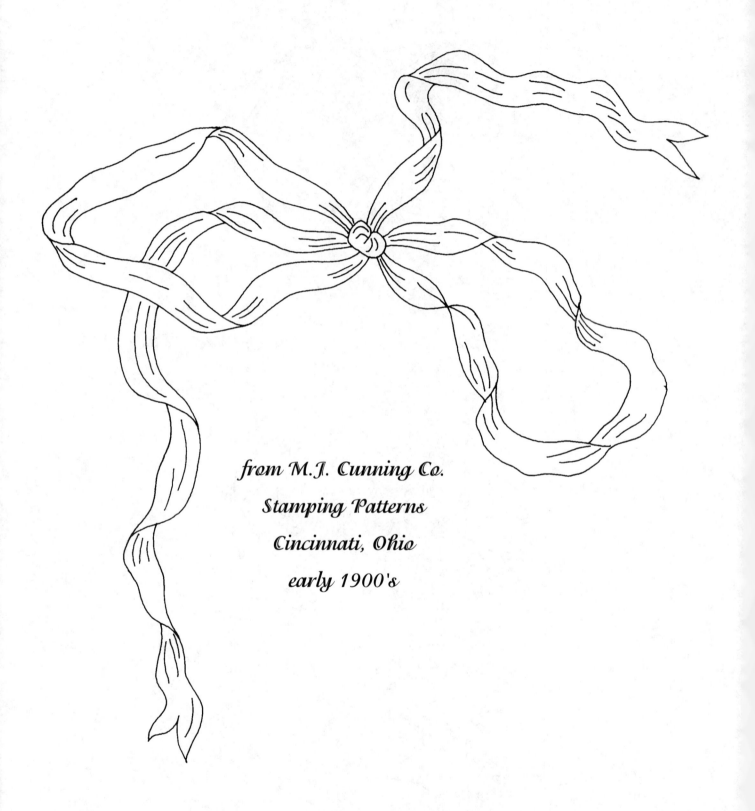

from M.J. Cunning Co.

Stamping Patterns

Cincinnati, Ohio

early 1900's

from John S. Piper
Stamping Patterns
Cincinnati, Ohio 1906

"Delsbo Embroidery is a Swedish art. It is simple, yet very artistic, and is adaptable for cushions, table covers, scarfs, etc. It takes its name from a small place in Sweden, called "Delsbo." The peasants dress in a national costume, rich in colors, and handsomely trimmed with silver buttons, braids, and highly colored ribbons. With its full skirts, unique headdress, fancy, striped apron, and the never missing handkerchief bag, fastened to the waist by a hand-woven ribbon, this costume is very fascinating to behold. Delsbo embroidery is worked in a flat, slanting Over and Over stitch. No padding is required. The designs are both the original and styleful, and not at all hard to execute. This oblong pillow cover is embroidered in Delsbo embroidery in old blue, old rose, and green, a combination which gains effectiveness from its rarity. The leaves are worked in green, the roses in two shades of old rose, and the scroll work is wrought in the old blue."

Designs for Towel Ends

- one half of the design -

center

from the Savannah Morning News - November 29, 1908

designed by Emma J. Buckman

centers of designs - one half of the design

Cutwork Linens

enlarge 200% - placemats

Needlecraft

The Home Arts Magazine

August, 1935   10¢

Patchwork for Coverlets - 4 Designs

enlarge 150%

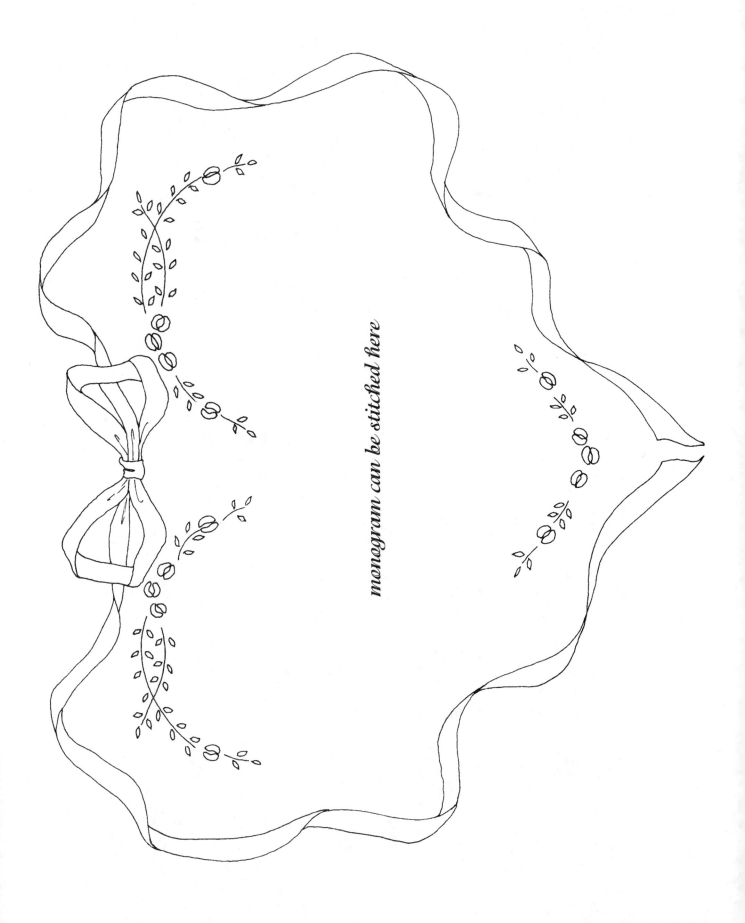

monogram can be stitched here

Grape Design
Used on Towel

Two-thirds
of Design,
Actual Size

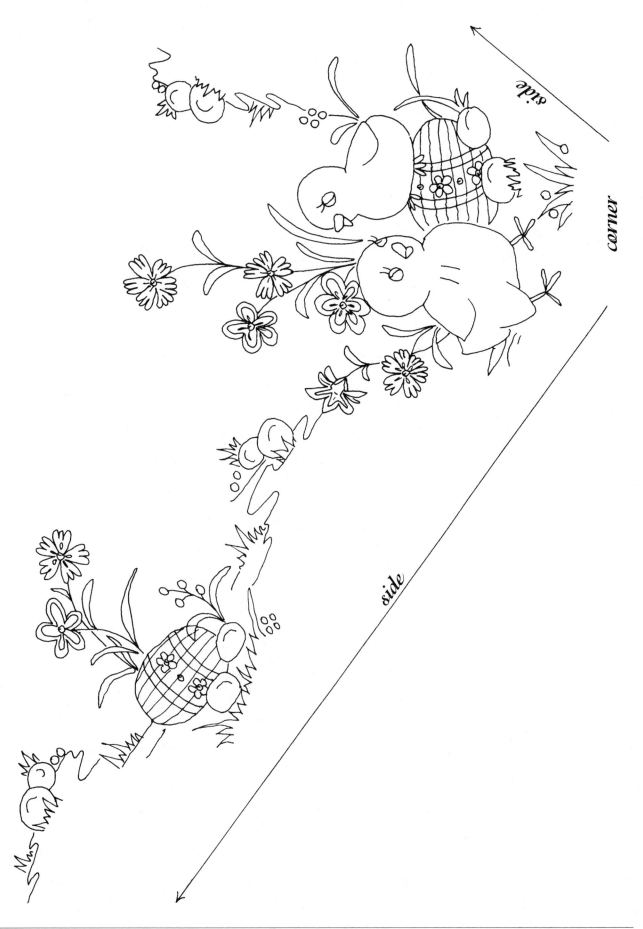

side

corner

side

Antique Embroidery

Designs

About Silk Ribbon Embroidery

About Silk Ribbon Embroidery

If you choose to embellish your special projects with silk ribbon you will find that it is actually much easier than it looks and it takes far less time than floss embroidery to complete a design. The craft of silk embroidery is little more than mastering a few basic stitches and using those stitches in combinations with each other. With a change in color and ribbon width, a basic leaf becomes a rose or a tulip. A French knot is babies' breath in one design and a rose or a hyacinth in another design simply by a change in the ribbon or number of twists on the needle. As you fill in your design you will find that silk ribbon is very forgiving and mistakes are easily corrected. You will become familiar with what works best for you as you play with different needles, ribbons and fabrics. We use YLI Silk Ribbons. They're gorgeous!

Fabrics

Many fabrics are suitable for embroidery; of course, some are easier to work with than others. All of the natural fiber fabrics are beautiful and very suitable. Some are cotton, linen, cotton velveteen, silk taffeta, raw silk, silk dupioni, natural silk and batiste. The following synthetic fabrics are also useful; moire taffeta, tapestry, lightweight polyester taffeta, organdy and satin. Experiment with several.

Needles

There are a variety of needles used for silk ribbon work, as you experiment, you will find what works best with which fabrics and stitches. Remember, the higher the size number, the smaller the needle.

Chenille Needle - A large, sharp pointed needle with a long eye. Sizes range from 18-24. Good for wide ribbon and tightly woven fabrics because it punctures a hole that will accommodate a wide ribbon.

Crewel Needle - This needle has a long eye and a sharp point. Sizes range from 1 to 10, however, sizes 3 to 9 are all you will ever need.

Tapestry Needle - A large eyed needle with a blunt end. It prevents snagging, and is great for passing through other ribbon; good for loosely woven fabrics. Sizes range from 13 to 26, with 18 to 26 being the most used.

Straw Needle - This needle is a long, narrow needle, also called a milliner's needle, which stays the same thickness from top to bottom. Which means the needle does not get fatter at the eye. This aspect makes it a great needle for French and colonial knots.

Darner - A very large eyed, long needle used for wide ribbons and heavy thick threads. Sizes range from 14 to 18.

Beading Needle - This needle is used for assembling roses, gathering stitches and tacking beads. It is a thin, long needle with a small eye.

Threading Silk Ribbon

For best results, work with ribbon no longer than ten inches at a time. The ribbon becomes frayed and hard to work with quickly, so if the ribbon is longer than ten inches, it will probably be wasted before it can be used.

To keep the needle threaded, insert the needle into the tail of the ribbon after it has been threaded through the eye of the needle (fig 1). Then, pull the tail back over the main ribbon so that it forms a loop (fig 2). Next, pull the main ribbon until the loop is closed (fig 3). This passes easily through the fabric and keeps the ribbon from coming unthreaded.

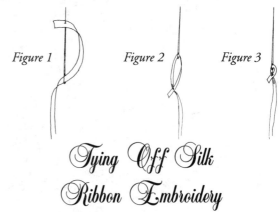

Figure 1   *Figure 2*   *Figure 3*

Tying Off Silk Ribbon Embroidery

There are two ways to tie on and to tie off the ribbon. One way is to simply tie knots. Knots are best for small projects. The second way is to leave about ¹/₂ inch of extra ribbon underneath the fabric, and when the needle is inserted back through to complete a stitch, insert the needle through the extra ribbon to secure it. When cutting the ribbon, leave an extra ¹/₂ inch and insert the needle through it when making another stitch. This method helps keep the back side free of so many knots, which can eventually get in the way when working a complicated design.

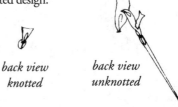

back view   back view
knotted   unknotted

Bearded Iris

1. With a 2mm, 4mm or 7mm ribbon, stitch a lazy daisy (fig. 1). Refer to the lazy daisy stitch in this section.

Figure 1

2. To create the beards, bring the needle up from under the fabric, below and slightly to the right side of the lazy daisy (fig. 2). Insert the needle behind the lazy daisy so that it does not catch the ribbon or the fabric and glides freely between them.

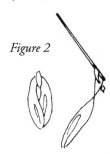

Figure 2

3. Pull the ribbon through and insert the needle into the fabric on the other side, below and to the side of the lazy daisy (fig 3).

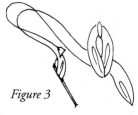

Figure 3

4. To complete this flower, add a twisted straight stitch for the stalk and a couple of long straight stitches for the leaves. NOTE: For added dimension, stitch the stalk and leaves first, and then add the iris tot the top of the stalk and allow the beards to lie on top of the leaves.

Bradford Rose

This rose is versatile. For variety, use a dark color for the center knot, a medium shade for the first round of wrapped stitches and a lighter shade for the outer row.

1. To begin this rose, make a colonial or French knot in the center (fig. 1).

Figure 1

2. Following the directions for a curved whip stitch on page 60, begin working clockwise around the center knot. Work three wrapped stitches for the first round (fig. 2).

Figure 2

3. Work four or five curved whipped stitches around the first round (figs. 3 & 4).

Figure 3

Figure 4

Bullion Rose

This ever popular rose embellishes the most elegant embroidery projects. It takes practice, but once the basic bullion stitch is mastered, all of the different bullion roses and flowers will be a cinch.

1. Bring the needle up from under the fabric at A and take a stitch down at B about 3/8" to 1/4" away from A, then come back up though A beside (not through) the ribbon. Do not pull the needle all the way through (fig. 1).

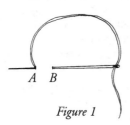

Figure 1

2. Now, hold the end of the needle down with your thumb. This will pop the point of the needle up away from the fabric. Wrap the ribbon coming from A around the needle 5 to 6 times, keeping the ribbon flat (fig. 2).

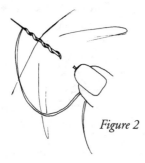

Figure 2

3. With your finger, push the wraps of ribbon to the bottom of the needle next to the fabric so that they are all lined up tightly (fig. 3). With your other hand, place your finger under the fabric and your thumb on top of the bullion and gently pull the needle and ribbon through the wraps (fig. 4).

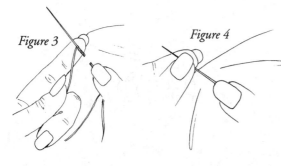

Figure 3   *Figure 4*

4. You almost have a bullion, but first you must lay the coils over to the opposite side and take up the slack ribbon (fig. 5). To do this, lay the bullion over and place your finger under the fabric and your thumb on top of the bullion, and gently pull the ribbon until the slack is out (fig. 6). Insert the needle into the fabric at the end of the bullion (fig. 7) and go on the next stitch, repeating the steps above. Refer to the template for stitch placement.

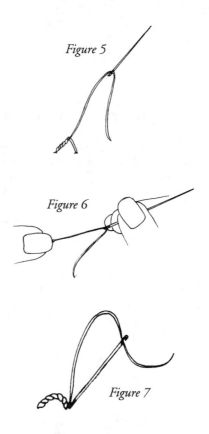

Figure 5

Figure 6

Figure 7

NOTE: The distance from point A to point B will determine the length of your bullion, and the number of ribbon wraps will determine the amount of curve. So, be sure you always have enough wraps to cover the distance.

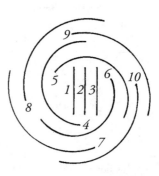

Bullion Rose Template

Bullion Lazy Daisy

Flowers and leaves take on a new dimension with this impressive looking silk ribbon stitch. This is a variation of the basic lazy daisy and bullion stitches. Review the lazy daisy instructions and the bullion instructions given for the bullion rose before beginning this stitch. This is the perfect stitch for the more exotic floral sprays. This stitch also makes wonderful leaves and is great used as a filler.

1. Start the stitch in the same manner as a lazy daisy. Instead of placing the ribbon behind the needle, wrap the ribbon around the needle two or three times, keeping the ribbon flat (fig. 1). Place your thumb on top of the bullion and hold between your thumb (on top of the fabric) and your finger (below the fabric) (fig. 2). Gently pull the needle and ribbon through (fig. 3).

| *Figure 1* | *Figure 2* | *Figure 3* |

2. Secure the stitch by inserting the needle down into the fabric at the end of the bullion (fig. 4).

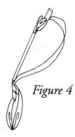

Figure 4

3. For added effect, change ribbon color and stitch a straight stitch or a Japanese ribbon stitch on top of each bullion lazy daisy (fig. 5).

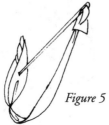

Figure 5

Buttonhole Stitch Flower

This wonderful stitch makes unusual flowers that have the appearance of hollyhocks. It is a good filler stitch when you need just something special to fill an area of a design. The buttonhole stitch flower is so easy and quick to do. I know you are going to love this stitch and the flowers you will be able to create with it.

1. The first stitch is a little different from the rest. I call this a starter stitch. Start on the perimeter of an imaginary circle at A. Take a stitch by inserting the needle into the center at B and out through C (fig. 1). Notice that C is just next to A for this first stitch. Wrap the ribbon over and around the needle and pull the ribbon through (fig. 2).

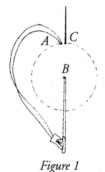
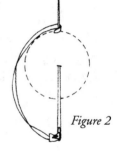

Figure 1

Figure 2

2. Now, to continue with the blanket stitch, insert the needle down into the center at B and make a stitch to the outer edge of the circle a short distance from the first stitch. Wrap the ribbon behind the needle (fig. 3) and pull through at D.

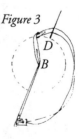

Figure 3

3. Repeat these steps, working from the center out all the way around. To end the circle, simply insert the needle down through the fabric at the top of the first stitch (fig. 4).

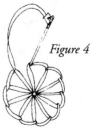

Figure 4

Buttonhole Stitch

This stitch is a beautiful way to outline the edge of an appliqué shape. It makes a great fence when used on an embroidered picture. When stitched in a circle, this stitch becomes a hollyhock or a pansy.

1. Bring the needle up through the fabric at A. Pull the ribbon above and to the right of A and hold it in place with your thumb (fig. 1).

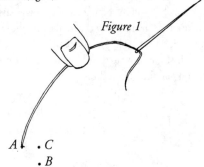

Figure 1

2. Insert the needle in B and up through C in one stitch, keeping the ribbon under the needle (fig. 2). Pull through.

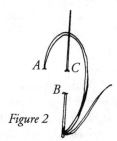

Figure 2

3. C now becomes A and the sequence repeats. You may see the sequence as A-B, A-B and on and on (fig. 3). Notice that the stitch looks like a series of upside down "L's".

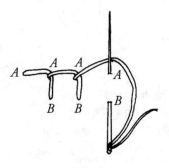

Figure 3

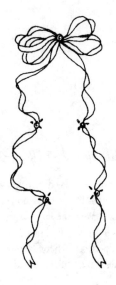

Cascading

This is a beautiful embellishment to add elegance and color when woven loosely through a floral design. It also secures and shapes the tails of a bow.

Bring the needle up through the fabric from underneath a bow or flower, or from wherever your streamers will be attached (fig. 1). Next, take a small stitch in the fabric about 1 inch or more away from where you came up and twist the ribbon so that it rolls and loops (fig. 2). Pull the ribbon very loosely and let it lie naturally. The loops may be tacked in place with French knots or seed beads.

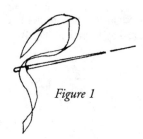

Figure 1

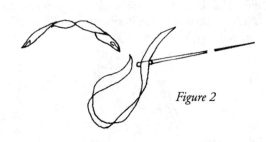

Figure 2

Cabbage Rose

Any project graced by this luxurious rose is instantly touched with a Victorian appeal. It is a wonderful ornament for hats, boxes, pillows and wedding dresses and veils. Technically, it is a variation of the hand wrapped rose. It is made exactly the same way only there is a twist at the end. It takes a little practice so don't be discouraged the first time.

1. Beginning with a flat piece of ribbon about 15 inches long, fold down about three inches at a right angle (fig. 1). Fold again, this time folding the ribbon back on itself. This will create a triangle in the corner (fig. 2).

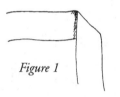 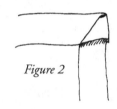

Figure 1   *Figure 2*

2. Place a pointed object such as the sharp tip of a chalk pencil or light colored pencil up through the "triangle" (fig. 3) and begin twisting with about two twists (fig. 4).

Figure 3   *Figure 4*

3. Begin folding the ribbon back while twisting the pencil (fig. 5). Continue folding and twisting until you have about 5 to 7 full twists for a full rose and about 4 twists for a small rosette.

Figure 5

4. Remove the rose from the pencil and hold it between your thumb and finger. Tack the bottom securely with a needle and thread, leaving the tails dangling (fig. 6).

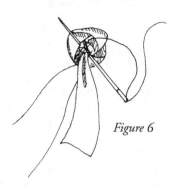

Figure 6

5. Now here's the tricky part, After you have tacked the rose to keep it from falling apart as you finish, take the tail of the ribbon and create loops as you would when making a Christmas bow (fig. 7). The point of the loop will be on bottom. Tack stitch each loop as it is formed to the bottom of the rose to secure it. Make four loops, one on each side of the rose. After the last loop, fold the raw edge under and stitch it securely (fig. 8).

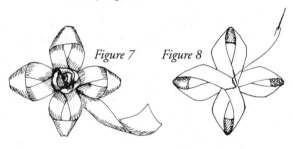

Figure 7   *Figure 8*

6. Pinch together the ends of the loop and take a couple of tiny stitches to secure (fig 9). Gently pull the tacked ends to the bottom center and take loose stitches to hold it in place. Tie a knot, then go to the next petal and repeat until all of the loops are tacked to the bottom. As you will notice, the tacked loops create puffy petals on the bottom of the rose and give the wrapped rose more volume (fig. 10).

Pinch the ends together and tack

bottom view

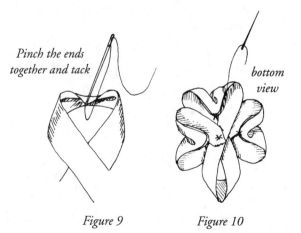

Figure 9   *Figure 10*

Chain Stitch

This is a glorified lazy daisy stitch that works beautifully on smocking and adds dimension to silk ribbon embroidery. It is a great outline stitch for stems and vines when done with one or two strands of floss.

1. Bring the needle up through the fabric at A. Swing the floss or ribbon around in a loop and hold the loop with your thumb (fig. 1).

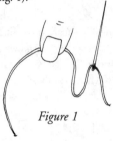

Figure 1

2. While holding the loop, insert the needle in at B and out through C in one stitch. Keep the needle and floss or ribbon going over the loop (fig. 2).

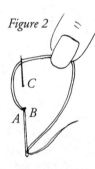

Figure 2

3. Instead of inserting the needle to the other side like a lazy daisy, you will make another loop and insert the needle down, right beside C where you came up, this will become a new A. In the same stitch, bring the needle through B and pull (fig. 3). Keep the needle over the loop.

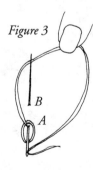

Figure 3

4. Continue looping and stitching in an "A, B" - "A, B" sequence.

Colonial Knot

Basic knot stitches are used in a variety of ways. They can be the centers of daisies or the blossoms of hyacinths. Colonial knots make beautiful grape clusters on a vine or tiny rosettes in a bouquet. The colonial knot differs from the French knot in the method of wrapping the floss or ribbon around the needle. It will also make a larger knot than the French knot. If you want the colonial knot to be "fluffy", do not pull the ribbon tight. The knot will "sit tall" on top of the fabric.

1. Come up from beneath the fabric and wrap the needle under the ribbon once (fig. 1).

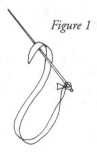

Figure 1

2. Next, wrap the ribbon over the needle once (fig. 2) and back under once (fig. 3). This makes a figure eight.

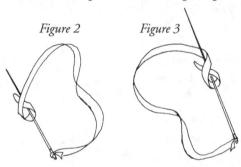

Figure 2   *Figure 3*

3. Insert the needle beside the original hole (fig. 4). While holding the needle vertically, pull the slack out of the ribbon so that the knot tightens around the needle (fig. 5). Continue holding the ribbon taut until the needle and ribbon have been pulled all the way through.

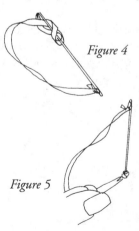

Figure 4

Figure 5

Concertina Rose

In my experience teaching silk ribbon. I have learned that not everyone can make a hand wrapped rose. The Concertina rose doesn't take quite so many fingers and toes to make, and it can stand in the place of a wrapped rose just as nicely on any project.

Once you try one of these roses, you will probably be reminded of decorating for the prom in high school - remember folding all that tissue? Well, this rose is done the exact same way. And if you've never folded tissue, try this technique the next time you have to decorate for a party!

1. Using 7mm or wider ribbon, cut a piece 12 to 14 inches long and fold it in half.

2. Start by folding the ribbon at a 90° angle (fig. 1). Fold the bottom ribbon over the top ribbon (fig. 2). Continue folding the bottom ribbon over the top until it has at least a 1 inch tail at the end (fig. 3).

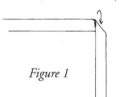

Figure 1

Figure 2

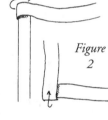

Figure 3

3. Hold the last folded edge of ribbon between your thumb and finger while your other thumb and finger pull the other ribbon tail gently until the folds have all collapsed on each other (fig. 4). You will see a rose forming from the top.

4. Stick a straight pin through the bottom to hold the rose while you tack it securely with a needle and sewing thread.

Figure 4

Couching

Couching is simply the attachment of ribbon or trim to fabric with tacking stitches. Couching is most often used as an edging method or to outline a shape. It is also very appropriate for silk ribbon smocking. Ribbon can be couched with other ribbon, silk thread, embroidery floss, pearls or beads. There are many variations of this concept. The ribbon can remain flat or it may curl or loop. Below are the general instructions for couching, along with the technique of couching with pearls.

1. The general technique is to make tack stitches over flat ribbon. Shape the ribbon to create a design or keep it straight as you would for covering a crazy patch seam. This tack stitch can be straight or angled. The angles can be in the same direction or different directions.

2. To start, bring the ribbon that is to be couched up through the fabric at an appropriate starting point and lay it flat in the direction you want it to be couched (fig. 1).

Figure 1

3. Thread a needle with ribbon or floss in a matching or contrasting color. Bring the needle up just beside the ribbon at the starting point of the flat ribbon in figure 1. Take a stitch over the ribbon to the other side (fig. 2). Continue wrapping the flat ribbon with the tack stitches, keeping them even in width and distance (fig. 3).

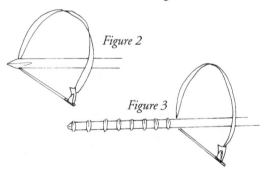

Figure 2

Figure 3

4. To couch with pearls, use regular sewing thread double threaded on a needle. Thread a strand of three pearls on each stitch (fig. 4). After each stitch, with a pointed object like the blunt end of a needle, pull up the flat ribbon to puff it.

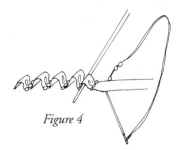

Figure 4

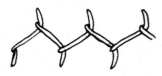

Cretan Stitch

The Cretan Stitch is a beautiful embellishment. This stitch is in the same family as the feather stitch. It takes a little practice at first, but if you have mastered the feather stitch, it will be no problem. For beginners, it helps to mark the points on your fabric to practice the stitch until you get the hand of it.

1. To begin this line of stitching, bring the needle up through the fabric at B. Insert the needle through A and back up through B again in one stitch. Wrap the floss or ribbon around behind the needle (fig. 1).

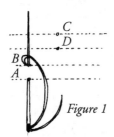

Figure 1

2. Pull the ribbon through and insert the needle through at C and D, keeping the needle over the floss or ribbon (fig. 2).

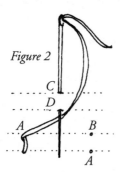

Figure 2

3. Repeat step 2 going in the opposite direction, inserting the needle in at A and up through B (fig. 3).

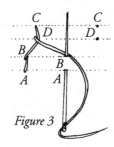

Figure 3

4. Continue repeating the A, B, C, D sequence and you will begin to see the pattern.

Fly Stitch

This stitch may be used for leaves at the base of flowers, it may be worked singly or in rows to give the appearance of ferns. This is an easy stitch to master and you will find many uses for it as fillers.

1. Come up at A. Insert the needle in the fabric at B, coming our of the fabric at C, making sure the loop of ribbon is below C (fig. 1). Keep the needle on top of the loop of ribbon.

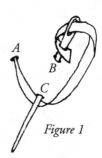

Figure 1

2. The length of the anchor stitch is determined by the length of the stitch taken between C and D. The floss or ribbon comes out of the fabric at C and the needle is inserted into the fabric at D. The longer the distance between C and D, the longer the anchor stitch. Gently pull the ribbon to the wrong side (fig. 2 & 3).

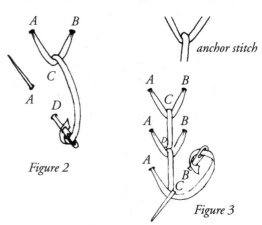

Figure 2

anchor stitch

Figure 3

Elongated Fly Stitch

The elongated fly stitch is the basic fly stitch worked with a longer anchor stitch. I like to use this stitch to form leaves at the base of buds and the elongated anchor stitch makes the stem for the flower. I can take care of two steps at one time by using this stitch.

Elongated Fly Stitch

Feather Stitch

This is a great embellishing stitch that is frequently used for stems and vines. You may add beads at the ends of the Y in the feather stitch for another variation.

1. Bring the needle up through the fabric at A (fig. 1). Insert the needle down about $^1/_4$ to $^3/_8$ inch across form A and into the fabric at B. In the same stitch, bring the needle out of the fabric $^1/_4$ to $^3/_8$ inch down and slightly to the right of center at C (fig. 2). With the ribbon behind the needle, pull the ribbon through (fig 3.). This stitch is much like the lazy daisy only the needle does not insert into the same hole in which it came up. Notice that the stitch is simply a triangle.

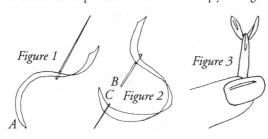

Figure 1   *Figure 2*   *Figure 3*

2. Now you will begin working your triangle from right to left, or left to right. C will now become A for your next stitch. Repeat the stitch as in step 1 (fig. 4).

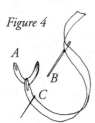

Figure 4

3. This time, repeat the stitch on the other side (fig. 5). The trick is that A and B will always be straight across from each other and that A, B and C will line up vertically (fig. 6).

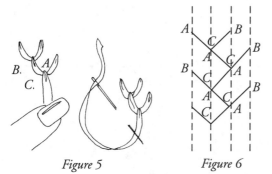

Figure 5   *Figure 6*

French Knot

This is one of the most versatile stitches that you will ever learn. The French knot is an easy stitch too use but it is one of the most intimidated stitches for embroiderers. The most asked question about French knot is "How many wraps?". The number of wraps will depend on the size of the knot desired, the type of thread or floss being used, and your personal preference. Generally, I recommend one strand of floss or 2mm silk ribbon with one to two wraps per knot. If a larger knot is needed, use more strands of floss or larger silk ribbon. Often times, French knots will not lay flat on the fabric. To eliminate this problem, once the needle has been reinserted in the fabric (fig. 3), slip the wrapped floss or ribbon gently down the needle until it rests against the fabric. Hold the wraps against the fabric and slowly pull the floss or ribbon through the wraps to the wrong side. This will cause the knot to be formed on the surface of the fabric and not float above it. Practice makes perfect and once this gorgeous stitch is mastered, you will find a million in one uses for it.

1. Bring the needle up through the fabric (fig. 1).

Figure 1

2. Hold the needle horizontally with one hand and wrap the ribbon around the needle with the other hand (fig. 2). If you are using a single stand of floss, one or two wraps will create a small knot. If you are making French knots with 2mm silk ribbon, the knot will be larger. As stated above, the size of the knot varies with number of strands of floss or the width of the silk ribbon being used.

Figure 2

3. While holding the tail of the ribbon to prevent it from unwinding off the needle, bring the needle up into a vertical position and insert into the fabric just slightly beside where the needle came out of the fabric (fig. 3). Pull the ribbon or floss gently through the fabric while holding the tail with the other hand.

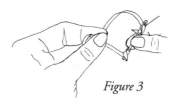

Figure 3

Hand Stitched Leaves

This leaf if perfect for large flowers where a lazy daisy, Japanese or straight stitch is inadequate. For best results, use a 7mm or wider ribbon.

1. Beginning with a flat ribbon about 6 inches long fold down one side at a right angle and leave about a 3 inch tail (fig. 1). Fold the other side the same so that the two sides meet edge to edge (fig. 2).

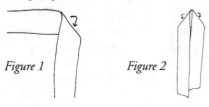

Figure 1   *Figure 2*

2. With a needle and thread, stitch across the flat edge of the ribbon (fig. 3a). For a slightly different look using the same technique, simply wrap the ribbon across itself instead of meeting edge to edge and stitch across (fig. 3b).

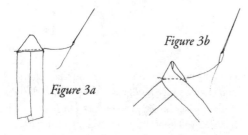

Figure 3b

Figure 3a

3. Pull the thread to gather the leaf. Wrap the thread around the stitching a couple of times to secure the gathers, then insert the needle through the ribbon and tie a knot (fig. 4).

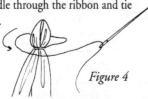

Figure 4

4. To apply the leaf to fabric, thread one of the dangling tails into a needle and insert into the fabric, pulling the ribbon to the back side. Repeat for the other tail and tie the tails together underneath (fig. 5). You may apply these before or after making a flower.

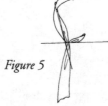

Figure 5

Herringbone Stitch

This beautiful line of stitching is a great decorative stitch. When doubled, this stitch becomes what Esther Randall calls a "Victorian stacking stitch". Use a 2mm ribbon for best results.

1. Bring the needle up at A. With the floss or ribbon on the right side of the fabric, make a long straight stitch from A to B (fig. 1). To practice, you may want to mark dots on your fabric and label each point until you get the hang of it.

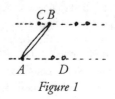

Figure 1

2. Bring the needle up through the fabric at C and make another long straight stitch to D (fig. 2).

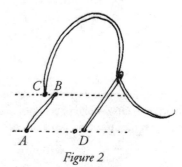

Figure 2

3. Repeats steps 1 and 2 and continue the A, B, C, D pattern (fig. 3). Notice the sequence of overlaps; the current straight stitch overlaps the previous stitch. Also, notice that the crosses are high and low, not in the center. This is controlled by the distance set between points C and B and point A and D when bringing your needle up through the fabric for the next stitch.

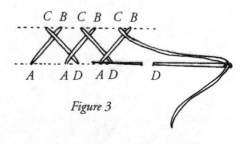

Figure 3

Hand Twisted Rose

This rose adds a wonderful dimensional appearance to any floral design and can be made in a variety of sizes.

Use a 7mm or wider ribbon to make this rose.

1. Beginning with a flat piece of ribbon about 15 inches long, fold down about three inches at a right angle (fig. 1). Fold again, this time folding the ribbon back on itself. This will create a triangle in the corner (fig. 2).

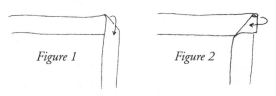

Figure 1   *Figure 2*

2. Place a pointed object such as the sharp tip of a chalk pencil or light colored pencil up through the "triangle" (fig. 3) and begin twisting with about two twists (fig. 4).

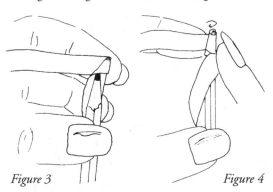

Figure 3   *Figure 4*

3. Begin folding the ribbon back while twisting the pencil (fig. 5). Continue folding and twisting until you have about 5 to 7 full twists for a full rose and about 4 twists for a small rosette.

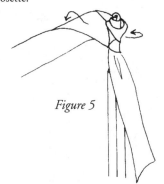

Figure 5

4. Remove the rose from the pencil and hold between your thumb and finger. Tack the bottom securely with a needle and thread, leaving the tails dangling (fig. 6). At this point, you may apply the rose to your project or you may make a fuller rose by gathering about $1^1/_2$ inch of the tail with a needle and thread (fig. 7).

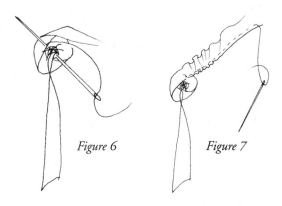

Figure 6   *Figure 7*

5. Wind this around the bottom of the rose and tack with the needle and thread (fig. 8).

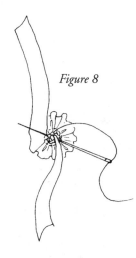

Figure 8

6. To apply the rose to fabric, thread one of the dangling tails into a needle and insert into the fabric, pulling the ribbon to the back side. Thread the other tail and insert underneath the rose into the fabric to the back side and tie the tails together (fig. 9).

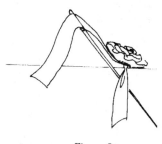

Figure 9

Japanese Ribbon Stitch

This stitch is simply a glorified straight stitch and may be used in as many variations. A rosebud is simply a Japanese ribbon stitch with straight stitches on both sides.

Use any size ribbon. Bring the needle up from under the fabric, loop it around and insert the needle down into the center of the ribbon a short distance in front of where the needle came up. Pull the ribbon so that the end curls in on itself loosely so that it does not disappear.

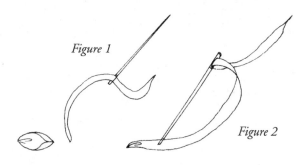

Figure 1

Figure 2

Leaf Ribbon Stitch

This versatile stitch is used for leaves and fern fronds. It also works well as leaves around small flowers or rosebuds.

1. Decide the length of the leaf or fern frond that you need and mark with a pencil or washout marker. As you begin to stitch, picture a leaf in your mind. It is narrow at the tip and becomes wider at the base. In order for the stitches to look like leaves or fern fronds, it will be necessary to gradually increase the width of the stitch.
2. Beginning at the top of the leaf, come up at A and go down at B. This will form a small straight stitch.
3. Come up at C and go down at D, bringing the needle out of the fabric at E and keeping D level with C.
4. Allow the needle to fall over the top of the ribbon loop.
5. Go down at F with a small straight stitch. This will anchor the stitch to the fabric.

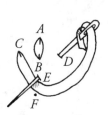

Lazy Daisy Stitch

This stitch is used in a variety of silk ribbon flowers and leaves. It is one of the most popular basic stitches.

1. Bring your needle up through the center point if you are stitching a flower, and up just next to a vine or flower for leaves (fig. 1).

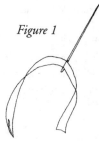

Figure 1

2. Insert the needle down into the same hole in which you came up. In the same stitch come through about $^1/_8$" to $^3/_8$" above that point (fig. 2). Wrap the ribbon behind the needle and pull the ribbon through, keeping the ribbon from twisting (fig. 3).

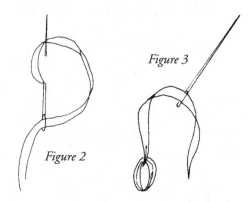

Figure 3

Figure 2

3. Insert the needle straight down into the same hole or very close to the same hole at the top of the loop (fig. 4). Notice in the side view of figure 4 that the needle goes down underneath the ribbon loop. The top view of figure 4 shows that the stitch is straight and will anchor the ribbon loop in place.

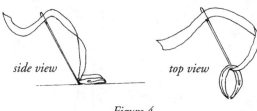

side view

top view

Figure 4

Loop Stitch French Knot

This is an unusual stitch that can be used as single flowers, grouped together or as a filler.

1. Come up at A and make a loop. Hold the loop in place with a pin.

2. Wrap the ribbon around the needle two times. Insert the needle at B, close to the pin. Gently pull the two wraps down the needle until they rest on the fabric. Holding the ribbon tight, gently pull the needle through the fabric forming a French knot (fig. 1).

Figure 1

B A

Loop Stitch

This stitch is to be made very loosely while keeping the ribbon straight. It can be used for daisies and bows or anywhere a loop look is needed. Experiment with different ribbon widths to achieve a variety of styles and uses.

Straight Stitch Method - Insert the needle up through the fabric and loop around away from you, inserting the needle just slightly beside where you came up (fig. 1).

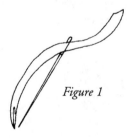

Figure 1

1. Pull the ribbon straight (without twists) and loosely adjust the loop to the desired size (fig. 2).

Straight Stitch Loop

Figure 2

Japanese Stitch Method - Insert the needle up through the fabric and this time loop it towards you, inserting the needle through the center of the ribbon just beside where the needle came up (fig. 3). Again, pull loosely while keeping the ribbon straight.

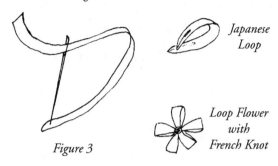

Japanese Loop

Loop Flower with French Knot

Figure 3

Pullen Knot

This stitch is a "mistake proof" stitch because it was created from an incorrectly formed French knot. It has proven to be a very versatile stitch that works great for floral clusters or simply as filler stitches. It adds so much depth and dimension to silk ribbon embroidery that you will find yourself using this stitch over and over again.

1. Bring the ribbon through the fabric at A and wrap the ribbon around the needle. The number of wraps depends on the size knot desired. Usually, from one to seven wraps is all that is needed. If you want a larger knot, simply use a larger ribbon. If you are doing a large number of wraps on the needle, it may be necessary to anchor the knot in place with monofilament thread after it is formed. The most important thing to remember about this knot is that all wraps must be kept loose on the needle.

2. Insert the needle into the fabric at B. When inserting the needle into the fabric, bring the needle as close to A as possible, but do not pierce the ribbon coming out at A. Pull the ribbon through the fabric but avoid pulling the stitch tight. The ribbon should be loose so that the knot appears to float on the fabric.

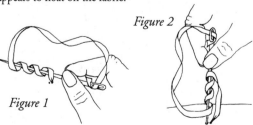

Figure 2

Figure 1

Pistol Stitch

This stitch may be used to form groups of flowers, flower centers or grass.

1. Come up at A. Allow a short length of the ribbon to extend above A. Keep the ribbon flat and taut (fig. 1).

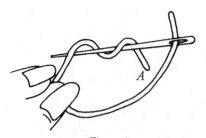

Figure 1

2. Wrap the ribbon around the needle two times. Insert the needle at B, gently pull the wrapped ribbon down the needle until it rests against the fabric. Hold the ribbon taut as you pull the needle through the fabric forming a two wrap French knot (fig. 2).

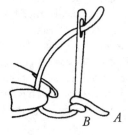

Figure 2

Finished
Stitch

Pansy

A few pearls or a French knot in the center of this flower will provide color, coverage and dimension. It is made by hand first and then tacked onto the fabric with a needle and thread, Four millimeter or wider ribbon works best.

1. Begin with a flat piece of ribbon $2^1/_2$ inches long. Fold one end at a right angle and stitch across the edge with a needle and thread. Fold the end (fig. 1).

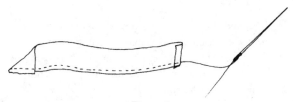

Figure 1

2. Pull the thread tightly to gather the ribbon (fig. 2).

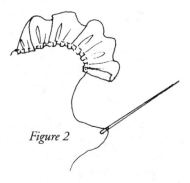

Figure 2

3. Curl the ribbon around so that the ends overlap. Tack the center with a couple of stitches to secure it and tie a knot (fig. 3). Tack to the fabric with thread and cover the center with pearls or a French knot.

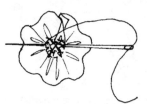

Figure 3

Petal by Petal Rose

This graceful, lifelike rose is appropriately named because each petal is literally made individually by hand before it is assembled into a rose. Janet Hyde taught me how to make this rose and though it is time consuming, it is more than worth the patience. It does appear to be difficult, but, it is truly easy to make and your friends will be so impressed.

This requires a 32mm ribbon. The petals vary in length and are prepared individually and then assembled from the smallest petals to the largest petals. A green wire edged ribbon bow is stitched to the bottom. Green silk leaves may be used instead of a bow.

Cut pieces of ribbon according to the following measurements.

       3 - 3" pieces (these will be the center)

       5 - 3 ¹/₂" pieces

       5 - 4" pieces

       5 - 4 ¹/₂" pieces

       5 - 5" pieces

       5 - 5 ¹/₂" pieces

Petal Directions

1. Fold the cut piece of ribbon in half and secure with a pin.
2. Fold in the corner of the folded end at an angle and roll toward the center of the ribbon (fig. 1). Whipstitch the roll in place, being careful to pick up only a thread or two so that the stitching does not show through to the other side of the petal (fig. 2).
3. Repeat this for the other corner so that the top of the petal is pointed (fig. 3).

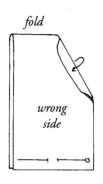

fold

wrong side

Figure 1

Figure 2

4. Make a tuck in the bottom at the raw edges of the ribbon and tack to secure (fig. 3).
5. Repeat these steps on all of the pieces of ribbon and set each petal aside until all of the petals are complete. Keeping the petals in separate piles will help when assembling the rose.

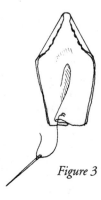

Figure 3

Assembling the Petals

1. Start with the smallest petal (this will be a 3" one) and curl it inward with the stitching to the inside. With a needle and thread, take a couple of tacking stitches and wrap the thread around the bottom to secure the curl (fig. 4).
2. Wrap another 3" piece around the curled petal and tack at the bottom (fig. 5). Complete the center by wrapping and tacking the last 3" piece.

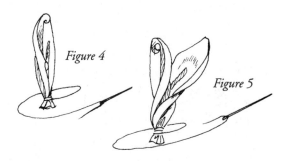

Figure 4

Figure 5

3. Continue layering and wrapping each of the 3 ¹/₂" petals (fig. 6). When the last 3 ¹/₂" petal is used, begin wrapping the 4" petals, then the 4 ¹/₂" petals, then the 5" petals, finishing with the 5 ¹/₂" petals and tacking as you go until they are all stitched together. When all the petals are stitched, take several stitches through all of the layers and then wind the thread around the bottom to secure.
4. As this point green silk leaves can be stitched to the bottom or a green wire ribbon bow can be tacked to the bottom as we have done on the sample (fig. 7).

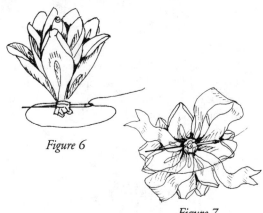

Figure 6

Figure 7

Ruching

Ruching is an age old technique seen on many antique garments. Most often strips of fabric were pleated, fluted or gathered to embellish women's and children's clothing. What we know as "puffing" was actually called ruching in the old days. In France, as ribbon became popular, it was used to adorn clothing as well. The ribbon was gathered or pleated and stitched directly on top of the garments since the edges were finished and raveling was not a concern. This particular "applied" typed of ruching is the technique we use with silk ribbon.

1. On a flat strip of 7mm or wider silk ribbon, run straight stitching, by hand or by machine, down the length of the ribbon to be gathered in a back and forth, zigzag direction (fig. 1). If hand stitching, it helps if you have a long beading needle, because you can get more tiny stitches on the needle before you have to pull the thread through.

Figure 1

2. Once stitching is complete, pull the thread to gather the silk ribbon (fig. 2). Gather as loosely or tightly as desired and tack with needle and thread or glue to project.

Figure 5

3. For a ruched carnation, simply coil the ruching. Gather the center tighter and loosen the gathering as you complete the outer petals (fig. 3), tacking with needle and thread as you coil.

4. For a ruched iris, roll the ruching up until you have rolled about five scallops. Pull two scallops up and three scallops down and wrap with thread. Tack to project and flare the petals (fig. 4).

Figure 4

Satin Stitch

The satin stitch is used to fill in an area with color by using heavy ribbon coverage. All of the stitches line up in the same direction creating a smooth, sometimes shiny appeal when it catches the light, looking like satin. To fill a given area takes patience because it is a slow moving stitch; the end result, however, is very pleasing.

1. It generally helps if you have the area to be filled traced on the project so that you have two definite lines to guide and maintain the varying width of the stitch as it fills different shapes. Secure in an embroidery hoop.

2. Begin at one end and work the needle from one side to the other, stacking the thread up just below and next to the previous stitch (fig. 1). Continue this wrapping process, keeping the fabric secured and taut while the stitches are pulled with light tension so that the fabric will not tunnel.

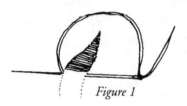

Figure 1

Running Stitch

1. Working from right to left, come up at A and go down at B.

2. Come up again at C making small, even stitches while working the needle into and out of the fabric. It is important that the stitches be kept the same length and that the distance between each space be consistent.

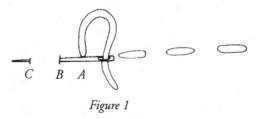

C   B   A

Figure 1

Silk Ribbon Weaving

Nothing is more elegant than a ribbon weave. Weaving ribbon adds surface interest to floral wreaths, and it's the perfect stitch to make baskets for silk arrangements. This technique is very easy and can be stitched in any shape. It is always done first, before the flowers are stitched.

Any size ribbon will make a weave, of course, it all depends on the size of your weaving shape. Once you get the hang of it, try different colors and different sizes together.

1. Trace the shape of the weave on the fabric. Begin at the top or the bottom of the shape and work to the other end. Bring the needle up through the fabric on one side of the traced line and insert it down through the fabric on the other side into the traced line (fig. 1). Keep the ribbon completely flat and smooth. If fraying occurs, switch to a bigger needle.

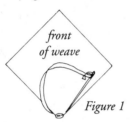

front of weave

Figure 1

2. Make the next stitch come up through the fabric next to the last inserted stitch (fig. 2) so that the back side becomes simply an outline of the shape and not covered with ribbon (fig. 3). In other words, you will not carry the ribbon across the back side of the fabric. When bringing the needle up for another stitch, allow room for the ribbon width. You want the ribbon edges to touch but not to overlap.

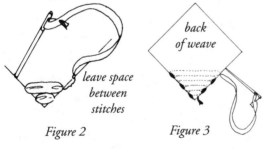

leave space between stitches

Figure 2

back of weave

Figure 3

3. Continue filling the shape with horizontal stitches following the shape of the traced lines.

4. Once the shape if filled with horizontal stitches, it is time to repeat the process vertically, only this time you will weave the ribbon through the horizontal ribbons before you insert the needle on the other side (fig. 4).

Figure 4

5. Tie off when complete and embellish the edges with flowers and leaves.

Spider Web Rose

This rose is one of the prettiest and easiest of all the silk ribbon stitched roses. Use 13mm for large puffy roses, 7mm for medium roses and 4mm for small roses. The spokes or "legs" on the spider will be shorter for 4mm ribbon than for 7mm ribbon. You will gain a good judgement for this after you have stitched a few roses and played with the different sizes.

Begin with a five legged "spider", or five spokes, stitched with either a single stand or a double strand of embroidery floss. For larger roses use a double strand. It may be helpful to mark a center with five evenly spaced dots around it using a washout pen or pencil as you are learning to make this rose.

1. To stitch the spider, come up from the bottom of the fabric with your needle through dot "a", then down in the center of dot "b" (fig. 1). Come up through "c", then down in "b" (fig. 2). Continue around; up in "d", down in "b", up in "e", down in "b" etc... until the spider is complete and tie off underneath (fig. 3).

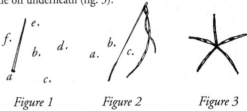

Figure 1   *Figure 2*   *Figure 3*

2. Now, with your silk ribbon, insert the needle up through the center "b" (fig. 4). Slide the needle under a spoke or "spider leg" and pull ribbon through loosely (fig. 5).

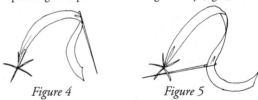

Figure 4   *Figure 5*

3. Skipping over the next spoke to under the third spoke (fig. 6) and begin weaving in a circle over and under every other spoke (fig. 7).

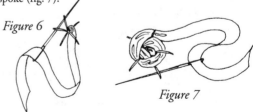

Figure 6

Figure 7

4. Continue weaving until the spokes are covered. Insert the needle underneath the last "petal" and pull through to the back.

You may stitch leaves first and then stitch the rose on top, or you may bring your needle up from underneath a "petal" and stitch leaves under the rose.

Split Stitch

This stitch is a very old embroidery stitch. It is customarily made using floss or a slightly heavier thread. It works well with silk ribbon.

1. Come up at A and go down at B, making a small backward stitch (fig. 1).

2. Come up at C piercing the ribbon in the center (fig. 2).

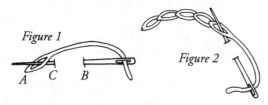

Figure 1

Figure 2

Stem/Outline Stitch

Worked from left to right, this stitch makes a line of slanting stitches. The thread is kept to the left and below the needle. Make small, even stitches. The needle is inserted just below the line to be followed, comes out to the left of the insertion point, and above the line, slightly.

1. Come up from behind at A and go down into the fabric again at B (fig. 1). This is a little below the line. Come back up at C (fig. 1). This is a little above the line. Keep the thread below the needle.

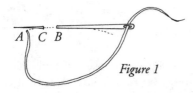

Figure 1

2. Go back down into the fabric at D and come up a little above the line at B (fig. 2)

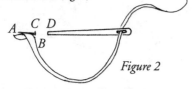

Figure 2

3. Continue working, always keeping the thread below the needle (fig. 3).

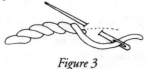

Figure 3

Straight Stitch

This stitch is used for almost everything. By itself or in combination with other stitches it becomes leaves, flowers, stems, vines, rose buds and more. Use any size ribbon. Narrow ribbons are good for vines, stems and tiny leaves, while wide ribbons are great for flower petals and big leaves.

Simply bring the needle up from under the fabric and insert it down into the fabric a short distance in front of where the needle came up. It is an in-and-out stitch. Remember to pull the ribbon loosely for nice full stitches.

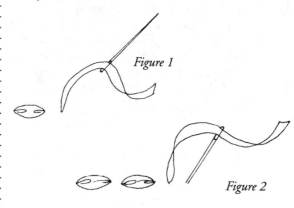

Figure 1

Figure 2

Twisted Loop

This stitch can be used to form loop flowers or as a filler. It will add dimension to any design you choose to use it on.

1. Come up at A and twist the ribbon (fig. 1).

2. Insert the needle at B and pull through the fabric, holding the loop in place with your thumb (fig. 1).

3. Insert the needle from the back at C, piercing the ribbon slightly above B (fig. 2).

4. Holding the loop in place with your thumb or a laying tool, make the next loop, being careful not to pull the previous loops out of shape (fig. 3).

Figure 1   *Figure 2*   *Figure 3*

Sweet Pea

Here is a dainty little flower to add to your floral bouquet. This one is so fun to make and can be made with several sizes of ribbon. Again, it is an individually hand-made flower that is later stitched to the project. The stitching on this flower is covered by the stem.

Sizes 7mm and 13mm ribbon are easiest to handle; however, for tiny projects a 4mm works well and looks like a blossom. For very large projects, a 32mm will create a huge carnation looking flower. Use a 7mm green ribbon for the flower base and leaves. Since sweet peas actually grow on vines, you may want to stitch a wrapped stitch vine before adding your flowers. This flower is not limited to being just a sweet pea, it can also be a poppy on its side or a carnation on its side by simply adding a stem. It's up to you.

1. Thread a needle with matching sewing thread and knot the end. Cut a piece of 7mm ribbon about 7" long. Use less for 4mm ribbon and more for 13mm ribbon. Fold each end to the center and fold the raw edges down (fig. 1). Pin to secure.

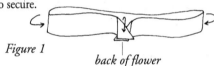

Figure 1   back of flower

2. With any stitches, run a gathering stitch across the bottom through both layers (fig. 2). Pull the thread to gather the ribbon and take a couple of tack stitches to secure (fig. 3).

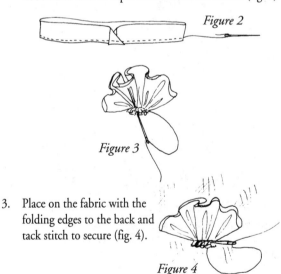

Figure 2

Figure 3

3. Place on the fabric with the folding edges to the back and tack stitch to secure (fig. 4).

Figure 4

4. Thread a 7mm green ribbon and make a straight stitch wrapping over the bottom of the flower to cover the tack stitches (fig. 5). This will also hold the sides of the flower up. Add leaves to complete.

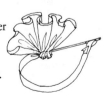

Tulip

With the appearance of tulips in the spring, everyone realizes that winter is almost over and the renewal of life is about to begin. Tulips are easy to make with silk ribbon. They are made using straight stitches and Japanese ribbon stitches. You may want to review these two stitches before beginning your tulips.

1. With a 4mm or 7mm ribbon, start by taking two small horizontal straight stitches (fig. 1).

Figure 1

2. Bring the needle up below and to the center of the previous stitches and make a vertical Japanese ribbon stitch to the left (fig. 2). Come up in the same center point and make another vertical Japanese ribbon stitch to the right (fig. 3).

Figure 2   *Figure 3*

3. Bring the needle up, once again, through the same center point and make a Japanese ribbon stitch between and on top of the two previous stitches (fig. 4).

Figure 4

4. Add a stalk and long straight stitch leaves to complete this beautiful spring flower. See finished drawing at top of page.

Wrapped Stitch or Wrapped Straight Stitch

This is a very effective stitch to use as a filler or to form stems for vines and flowers, seeds, small buds or roses. It is a simple stitch but will add so much to the overall look of the design.

Single

1. Keep the ribbon flat.

2. Come up at A, go down at B, making a straight stitch the length needed.

3. Bring the needle up again at A. The straight stitch just made should be flat on the fabric but not tight (fig. 1)

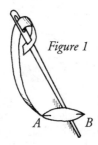

Figure 1

4. Slip the needle underneath the ribbon (fig. 1), making sure that you do not catch the fabric with the needle, gently pulling the ribbon around the straight stitch previously made. Do not allow the ribbon to twist (fig. 2).

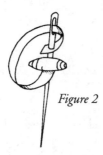

Figure 2

5. The number of wraps will depend on the desired effect you want your design to have and the length of your straight stitch. Most of the stitches are wrapped 2 or 3 times. If you want a thicker wrapped stitch, simply wrap more times (fig. 3).

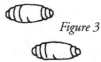

Figure 3

6. To tie off the stitch, slip the needle through the fabric to the wrong side and tie off.

Curved Whip Stitch

This stitch works wonders when used in a silk ribbon project.

1. Keep the ribbon flat. Come up at A, go down at B, making a straight stitch the length needed.

2. Bring the needle up again at A. The straight stitch just made should be flat on the fabric but not tight (fig. 1).

Figure 1

3. Slip the needle underneath the ribbon at b, making sure that you do not catch the fabric with the needle. Gently pull the ribbon around the straight stitch just made, pulling in the direction of "a". Wrap the stitch two or three times inserting the needle under "b" and coming out at "a". Make sure that you "squeeze" the stitch to make it curve (fig. 2).

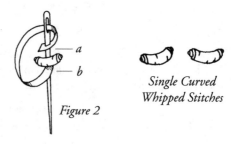

Figure 2

Single Curved Whipped Stitches

Interlocking Curved Whipped Stitch

The interlocking curved whipped stitch is referred to in several of the designs in this book. As you see, this simply means that the stitches will face each other like puzzle pieces that are being fitted together.

Interlocking Curved Whipped Stitches

Whipped Running Stitch

This stitch is used for vines, stems and stalks. Use a 2mm or 4mm ribbon. You may also use embroidery floss.

1. Stitch a line of straight stitches along the design line (fig. 1). Refer to straight stitch instructions.

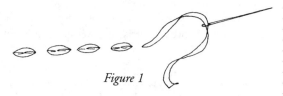

Figure 1

2. Bring the needle up at the end of the line of straight stitching (fig. 2).

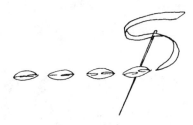

Figure 2

3. Begin wrapping the ribbon under and around the straight stitches (fig. 3).

Figure 3

Wisteria

This blossom is simply a cluster of colonial or French knots arranged in a loose triangular shape. Keep in mind that wisteria grows on a vine. So, stitch the vine first and add the blossoms and leaves later.

1. It is a good idea to mark dots on your fabric to create the shape of the cluster when you are learning to make this blossom (fig. 1). Once comfortable with the concept, dots are no longer needed as a guide.

Figure 1

2. Refer to the French knot or colonial knot instructions if necessary. Starting at the top of the blossom (this is the thickest part of the cluster), stitch plump knots by wrapping the needle two or three times with a colonial knot and four or five times with a French knot. As you work down the cluster, reduce the number of wraps to two and three. As you reach the bottom, the last three or four knots should be wrapped once or twice (fig. 2).

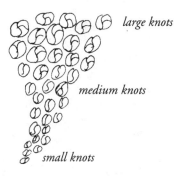

large knots

medium knots

small knots

Figure 2

This blossom can also be made entirely out of the same size knot. Try both ways and choose your favorite method.

3. To complete the blossom, add a small, twisted, straight stitch stem and a couple of Japanese ribbon stitch leaves.

Twisted Chain

To create a truly luscious rosebud, use 7mm ribbon and this stitch. The wrapped effect it gives makes the rosebud more realistic. When making large roses, this stitch and 7mm ribbon used to form leaves will prevent the leaves from becoming lost in the design. It truly is a versatile stitch that you will find hundreds of uses for.

1. Bring the ribbon or floss up at A and form a loop (fig. 1).

Figure 1

2. Hold the loop in place and insert the needle through the fabric at B, slightly to the left of A and out at C (fig. 2). Make sure that the ribbon or floss is underneath the needle at C.

Figure 2

Straight Stitch Rose

A straight stitch rose is simple and easy to make. Refer to the instructions given for a straight stitch in this section.

1. Work 3 French knots or Colonial knots in the center (fig. 1).

2. Work 3 straight stitches in a triangle around the center French knots. The straight stitches need to partially cover the stitch before (fig. 2).

3. Continue making rows of straight stitches being careful to overlap the stitches slightly as you work around the rose. The size of the rose is determined by the number of rows worked (fig. 3).

Figure 1   *Figure 2*

Figure 3

Stem Stitch Rose

A stem stitch rose is a quick and easy flower to make. The rose begins with French knots in the center. The rows of stitches that follow are simple stem stitches worked in a circle. The more rows of stem stitches worked, of course, the larger the rose will be. You may shade this rose by making each row of stitches a lighter color. It will give the flower a more realistic look. As you stitch, you will notice the stitches are overlapping each other filling in all areas.

1. Work a small cluster of French knots for the center of the rose. You may want to review the French knot instructions given in this section (fig. 1).

2. Begin the first row of the rose by working loose stem stitches counter clockwise around the knot. Bring the ribbon up at A, insert the needle in at B and out again at C, making sure that the ribbon or floss is underneath the needle (fig. 2).

3. The stem stitches will need to be made longer with each round of stitches that you make.

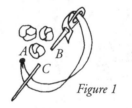   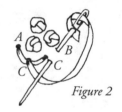

Figure 1   *Figure 2*

Twisted Straight Stitch

This stitch makes a lovely addition to the normal straight stitch and the only difference is a deliberate twist in the ribbon. Let your imagination dictate where to put this stitch.

1. Following the instructions given for the straight stitch, bring the ribbon up at A and twist in one time, going back into the fabric at B (fig. 1).

2. Allow the twisted straight stitch to sit on top of the fabric. If pulled tightly against the fabric, you will loose the curl of the ribbon (fig. 2).

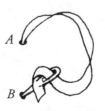   

Figure 1   *Figure 2*

Loop Stitch with French Knot Anchor

This stitch is one of the more versatile stitches in silk ribbon embroidery because of its many uses. If using larger ribbon, the ribbon takes on the look of a bow. If you want to make a stem of flowers, it will work for the flowers on either side of the stem. It is also great used simply as a filler.

1. Following the instructions for the loop stitch, complete the loop of ribbon (fig. 1). Make sure that you keep the loop larger than normal.

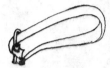

Figure 1

2. Flatten the loop until it is centered between A and B. Bring the needle up between A and B, piercing the flat ribbon (fig. 2).

A   B

Figure 2

3. Using the instructions for a French knot, work a single wrap French knot in the center of the ribbon (fig. 3).

Figure 3

4. Pull the French knot until is rests tightly against the ribbon. The French knot serves as an anchor for the ribbon loop (fig. 4).

Figure 4

Twisted Chain Stitch Rose

This stitch makes a beautiful rose that makes one feel they are looking down on the rose. If you need a quick and easy rose for a project, this would be the stitch to use. Keep in mind that when a rose opens, the center is always tighter than the last row of petals. As you finish the center stitches of the rose, the stitches should gradually become looser as you progress to the outer row of petals. The size of the rose is determined by the number of rows worked.

1. Work a French knot or Colonial knot in the center.

2. Come up at A beside the knot and wrap the ribbon around the knot counterclockwise (fig. 1). Remember, when beginning a stitch, stay as close to the previous petal as you can to avoid holes in the flower. Insert the needle at B, close to the knot and take a small stitch coming up at C, next to the knot (fig. 1).

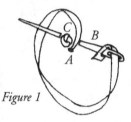

Figure 1

3. Pull your ribbon toward yourself until taut. Wrap the ribbon around the knot counterclockwise. Repeat the instructions given in step 2 for stitches 2 and 3 (fig. 2).

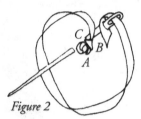

Figure 2

4. Continue working the stitches in a circle until you have the size rose desired (fig. 3).

5. To complete the last stitch, pierce the fabric angling the needle toward the rose.

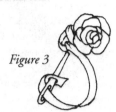

Figure 3

About
Martha Campbell Pullen, Ph.D.

Martha Campbell Pullen didn't invent heirloom sewing — the art of joining laces to create fabric has survived for centuries — but she and her fabulous staff can take some of the credit for turning this age-old art into a hobby that's approaching "all the rage" proportions.

Pullen personally learned how to smock and French sew by machine over 20 years ago when she was making clothes for her baby daughter. She realized if she could be drawn in so passionately, other women could be as well.

Today, she fronts her own heirloom sewing empire, which grew out of a tiny shop in Huntsville, Alabama. In 1981, two months after opening that shop, she began importing laces and fabrics to sell mail-order both wholesale and retail. Next, came Martha Pullen Heirloom Sewing Schools, which now attract more than 600 women to Huntsville twice a year. Their success prompted Pullen to venture out of her local market, conducting full scale Martha Pullen schools in Australia, England, Sweden, Canada, New Zealand and Texas. She has done mini-schools in almost every state in the United States.

An accomplished author, she has more than 25 books to her credit including three hardback manuals in excess of 400 pages. "Hobby to Profit with Grace," her most recent book is being published by Broadman and Holman, an arm of the Baptist Sunday School Board. It will be in Christian and mainstream bookstores nationally.

Adding to that list of successes, and probably the project of which she is most proud, is *Sew Beautiful*, a magazine she founded and began publishing over a decade ago. The publication focusing on heirloom and other classic sewing arts has an international following and distributes in excess of 90,000 copies bi-monthly. Four years ago, she began sharing her love of heirloom sewing with public television audiences around the country through her *Martha's Sewing Room* series.

To encourage heirloom sewing in cooler climates, Pullen expanded the range of materials used from traditional batistes and other lightweight materials to wool challis, corduroys, flannels and home dec fabrics. She has even come up with a name for these garments — love clothes.

"I call them 'love clothes' because I quickly realized that they are the special garments we make with love for the people we love," she explained. "With sewing, it almost seems that the love goes right from the machine or stitching needle into whatever we are making, especially where children are involved. It means so much more than just purchasing something ready made. Best of all, the classic, beautifully-sewn heirloom garments can carry that love from one generation to another."

Annually, Pullen presents *Martha's Sewing Market* at the Arlington Convention Center in Arlington, Texas. Her consumer exhibitions feature top international sewing instructors, more than 50 class choices per day, a vendor arena, fashion shows, and displays.

"Sewing makes memories that are passed on from generation to generation through the actual garments but also through the stitches learned," said Pullen, who is on the road promoting the art of sewing many weeks out of every year.

A native of Scottsboro, Alabama, Pullen is an internationally-known lecturer and teacher in the heirloom sewing field. After graduating with a degree in speech and English from the University of Alabama, she taught those subjects at almost every level of middle school and high school. Later, her studies led to a Ph.D in educational administration and management from the University of Alabama.

She has been named Huntsville Madison County Chamber of Commerce Executive of the Year, the second woman in the history of the organization to receive this award. She has been a nominee for *Inc,* magazine's executive of the year. She is a member of Rotary International and Optimist International. She has served on the board of directors of the Smocking Arts Guild of America and has presented workshops in French sewing by machine throughout the United States, Australia, England, Canada, Sweden and New Zealand. She is the wife of Joseph Ross Pullen, an implant dentist and president of her company, mother of five, grandmother to eight, with two more on the way! An active member of her church, she also volunteers with the Southern Baptist International Mission Board.